Philemon

Philemon

The Fourth Pastoral Epistle

Phil Nason

Copyright © 2015 by Phil Nason.

ISBN:	Softcover	978-1-5035-8982-7
	eBook	978-1-5035-8981-0

All rights reserved. No part of this book may be reproduced or transmitted in any form or by any means, electronic or mechanical, including photocopying, recording, or by any information storage and retrieval system, without permission in writing from the copyright owner.

Scripture quotations marked KJV are from the Holy Bible, King James Version (Authorized Version). First published in 1611. Quoted from the KJV Classic Reference Bible, Copyright © 1983 by The Zondervan Corporation.

Any people depicted in stock imagery provided by Thinkstock are models, and such images are being used for illustrative purposes only.
Certain stock imagery © Thinkstock.

Print information available on the last page.

Rev. date: 07/27/2015

To order additional copies of this book, contact:
Xlibris
1-888-795-4274
www.Xlibris.com
Orders@Xlibris.com

CONTENTS

Introduction: 1
   a. The Pastoral Epistle Question 1
   b. Authorship 3
   c. Which Imprisonment is Paul suffering? 5
   d. Is the church in the letter to Philemon the same church in the letter to the Colossians? 7
   e. Onesimus, Slave or Son? 10

I. Greeting: Vss. 1-3 17
   a. Paul, a prisoner 17
   b. Philemon 18
   c. Timothy 20
   d. The house-church 20
      1. Apphia 20
      2. Archippus 21
   e. Paul loves the church 23

II. Prayers for Philemon vss. 4-6 25
   a. Paul is Thankful 25
   b. Paul points to the Builder's Tools 26
   c. Paul shows there is Power in the Church 27

III. For Love's Sake vss. 7-9 29
   a. The Foundation to all Reconciliation is Love. 30
   b. Paul could be Bold 31
   c. To Build is not always to use a Hammer 33

IV. Paul Makes His Request Known vss. 10-14 35
    a. Onesimus 35
    b. Being Profitable 38
    c. Refresh my heart, Receive him. 39
    d. The Obligation of Service 41
    e. It is Better to Want than to Need 43

V. There is a Reason to Everything vss. 15-17 45
    a. Time and Times 45
    b. Onesimus, once the Slave 47
    a. Onesimus, now the partner 49

VI. Paul Addresses Consequences vss. 18-20 50
    a. Balancing some Books 50
    b. Balancing the Right Books 55
    c. Do the Right Thing 58

VII. Looking Ahead Together vss. 21-24 59
    a. "Having confidence in thy obedience. . ." 60
    b. Paul's Plans 61
    c. Epaphras 63
    d. Supporting Companions of Paul 64
        1. Mark 65
        2. Aristarchus 66
        3. Demas 66
        4. Luke 67
    e. Sincerely yours 68

APPENDIX A. 71
    Personal translation of the book of Philemon.
        Not to be used in public worship. 71

APPENDIX B. 73
    Opening address identifications of Paul as found in
        his 12 books of the NT. 73

APPENDIX C 74
    Sermon: From Slave to Beloved Brother 74

BIBLIOGRAPHY 83

PART ONE: EXPOSITION

INTRODUCTION:

The Pastoral Epistle Question

What makes a letter from Paul a Pastoral Epistle? I first asked this question concerning Philemon when I noticed that some commentaries pertaining to 1 and 2 Timothy and Titus contained work on Philemon, and some did not. Philemon seemed to be a "red-headed stepchild." It is a short, personal, and uniquely styled letter. It didn't seem to fit into any category neatly. Some commentators classify this work as a Prison Epistle simply because it was a letter written by Paul while he was in prison. H.A. Ironside defines Pastoral Epistle as a letter, ". . . written to servants of Christ who, in a very special sense, had the care of God's people in different places."[1] Donald Guthrie in the introduction to his book on the Pastoral Epistles states, "All three Epistles (*1and 2 Timothy, and Titus*) are directed to individuals, and many of the injunctions are clearly personal. Yet much of the material appears to be designed for the communities."[2] From these sources

---

[1] H.A. Ironside, *1 and 2 Timothy, Titus, and Philemon* (Grand Rapids: Kregel Publication, 2008), 9.

[2] Donald Guthrie, *The Pastoral Epistles* (Grand Rapids: Wm B. Eerdmans Publishing Company, 1990), 17.

and from reading the letters of Paul, a working definition of what constitutes a Pastoral Epistle can be formulated. A Pastoral Epistle needs to be written to an individual, and it needs to instruct the whole church in matters of faith and practice.

It does not matter in what situation Paul found himself when he wrote these letters. Paul was in prison when he wrote 2 Timothy and Philemon. He wrote 1 Timothy and Titus when he was free to travel unencumbered. Some might argue that because Philemon was not the Pastor of the church this letter could not be a Pastoral Epistle. While it is true that Philemon was not the pastor of the church by election or selection, he was a lay-pastor of the church by the virtue of his participation and life within the church family (*vs. 7*). The church met in his house (*vs. 2*). He most probably funded the church heavily (*vs. 6*). He was a man of incredible influence in the church (*vs. 21*). It is interesting that Paul, in fact, did not write to Archippus, the pastor of the church, directly to instruct him (*vs. 2*). Every pastor in any church knows of those lay people who are *de facto* pastors of their congregation; those who exercise incredible influence without an official position. Philemon was that *de facto* pastor. In the truest sense, then, this is a letter to a pastor of the church.

I come now to the issue of a Pastoral Epistle having to do with church matters. 1 and 2 Timothy and Titus deal with defining doctrine and setting order in the church through the use of official positions or hierarchy in the church. Philemon does not explain doctrine, nor does it call for the ordination of an elder or outline how the men and women should relate to one another in church. However, Philemon is addressing the whole church (*vss. 2, 3, 6, 22*). It would be inconceivable that a few verses would be read to the congregation at the beginning and the end of the letter without also reading the middle. Therefore, what Paul was writing to Philemon was to be heard by and to be applied to the whole congregation. Paul wanted to bring about order in the church by their service to the law of love. As Philemon is instructed to love Onesimus, the church is also instructed to love one another. This also puts the spotlight on love as the doctrine taught in this letter. While the other Pastorals teach about doctrines, Philemon puts the human face on this doctrine. Paul talks about love throughout his collected works, and in this letter he says, "This is what love looks like in action." Philemon passes the test, therefore, for being a Pastoral Epistle. It is written to an individual as Timothy and Titus were, and it guides the whole church in a proper use of their faith.

Authorship

With the letter to Philemon we have a most interesting situation. It is almost universally undisputed that Paul wrote this short letter. John Knox of Union Theological Seminary writes in his introduction to

Philemon as part of The Interpreter's Bible Series, "No reputable modern scholar doubts its authenticity. The little letter bears in itself every mark of genuineness. Its vocabulary and style are those of Romans, Corinthians, Galatians, and Philippians; and the personality of its author is unmistakable."[3] What is interesting about this consensus is that, in contrast, the other books of the Bible that are commonly identified as written by Paul are widely disputed.

With this agreement that Philemon is absolutely by Paul, there is a domino effect evident on the authenticity of the other disputed books. There are some theologians who question that Paul wrote Colossians. However, since it is taken as true that Paul wrote Philemon then it must also be taken as true that Paul wrote Colossians due to the commonality of the two letters. Read, for instance, the fourth chapter of Colossians to see the people in their proper roles paralleled to Philemon. Furthermore, it stands to solid reason that since Paul wrote Colossians then Paul also wrote Ephesians due to the common message and doctrine presented. Once Ephesians is substantially verified as penned by Paul, it is not a giant leap to find all the other epistles traditionally accepted to be authentic to Paul.

God has provided to those who look for it the mark of authenticity within this letter that some have even questioned should

---

[3] *The Interpreter's Bible*, s.v. "Introduction to Philemon."

be included in the canon of the New Testament. J. Vernon McGee stated a common view of many people in our pews, "Frankly, I believe that Paul had no idea his letter to Philemon would be included in the canon of Scripture, and I think he would be a little embarrassed."[4] My wife likes to go to doll shows. She is an avid collector with a fine collection of modern and antique dolls. Often the provenance of a doll she is looking at is in dispute. She cannot always tell just by looking at the face of the doll who the manufacturer may be, the date of origin, or the value of the doll. However, by looking at the back of the neck, underneath the hairline, there is often some sculptor's mark. This mark might be initials, or it might be a small design. By this simple mark the entire provenance of the doll can be deciphered, thereby establishing the overall value of the doll. In this one 25 verse letter, The Holy Spirit has provided the mark of authenticity for the entire collection of the letters of Paul.

Which Imprisonment is Paul suffering?

The fact that Paul was in prison is also an area of universal agreement. He states this point clearly in verses 1, 9, 13, and 23. But the question becomes which prison and which time? Acts 24 begins with Paul on trial before Felix, the Governor in Caesarea, for being a "pestilent

---

[4] J. Vernon McGee, *First and Second Timothy, Titus, Philemon* (Nashville: Thomas Nelson Publishers, 1991), 179.

fellow, and a mover of sedition among all the Jews throughout the world, and a ringleader of the sect of the Nazarenes:" (*vs. 5*) After two years of incarceration there and refusing to pay a bribe to Felix for his freedom, Festus replaced Felix as Governor (*vs. 27*). Before Festus, Paul appealed his case to Caesar in Rome, as recorded in Acts 25:11-12. Acts 26 ends with Paul's journey to Rome being decreed by King Agrippa. Therefore, for over two years, Paul had the time to write Colossians and Philemon, but not the holy inspiration. In Philemon, Paul anticipates an opportunity to come to visit Philemon, visit that church, and to be refreshed. He asks for lodging (*vs. 22*). He sends some of his companions ahead to prepare the way because he believes that the time is at hand (*vss. 23-24*). From Caesarea, however, Paul anticipated going to Rome to be heard before Caesar due to his appeal. This is quite a difference in travel itineraries.

This leaves the most plausible imprisonment to be the two years that he spent under house arrest as recorded in Acts 28:30-31. During these years, he received guests, preached, and taught. The final words of the book of Acts even include, ". . . with all confidence, no man forbidding him." (*vs. 31c*). This would provide ample opportunity for Paul to communicate with the churches and individuals freely. Buttressed by King Agrippa's recommendation for freedom (*Acts 26:32*), Paul came to expect that he would one day be set free to travel again, and that Nero would be a reasonable judge. From AD 60-62, during the first Roman imprisonment, this proved to be the truth of the matter. Therefore, the date of the letter to Philemon, as well as the letters to the Ephesians, Philippians, and Colossians, can best be placed at, or close to, AD 62.

Is the church in the letter to Philemon the same church in the letter to the Colossians?

The letters to the Colossians and to Philemon are two parts of the same message. The fourth chapter of Colossians is essential as an introduction to Philemon. Many commentators on the Bible include Philemon with their work on Colossians, rather than with the two letters to Timothy and Titus. It may be surmised, then, that the congregation meeting at Colosse and the house church of Philemon are one in the same. This assumption, however, would not be accurate. While both letters were written at the same time, and to the same geographic area, they are to be carried to two different places. Colossians 4:7-8 states that Paul is sending Tychicus to the Colossians as a pastor. In fact, Tychicus is to be accompanied by Onesimus, "a faithful and beloved brother, who is one of you. . ." (*vs. 8*). However, there is no mention of Tychicus in the letter to Philemon either as a member of the house church or as coming with the other travelers listed at the end of the letter. It would be unlikely that Paul would address the church in the letter to Philemon without mention of Tychicus if he were part of it in some way. To mention Onesimus so highly in Colossians is to affirm that Paul anticipated a happy resolution to the crisis of departure and restoration contained in Philemon. He also identified Onesimus as being one of them. Therefore, two things are possible and one of them is probable. The possible things are (1) Colosse had at least two house churches going on at the same time, or (2) the church at Colosse maintained a close personal relationship with the house church of Philemon at another location.

Seeing as house churches are by nature smaller congregations, it seems unlikely if there were two house churches in one town that Paul would be addressing both with equal honor without calling for a unification of efforts. Neither Colossians nor Philemon carries such a call to unite under one roof. Certainly one larger church can carry on the evangelistic efforts in a small city more effectively than two separate congregations, unless the churches have different demographics or divergent doctrines. There is no evidence of that here. The detail of doctrinal statement contained in the letter to the Colossians as contrasted with the brevity of the letter to Philemon seems to indicate that the Colossian church was the larger or more developed congregation.

The second possibility is also the one probability. The churches are separate, but they share common bonds. This leads to the probability that the church in the letter to Philemon was what we might call today a mission of the church in Colosse. Colossians 4:17 records words that are reminiscent of what a sponsoring church might say to a pastor they are commissioning to do the work of a mission, "And say to Archippus, 'Take heed to the ministry which thou hast received in the Lord, that thou fulfill it.'" Tychicus is the pastor to the church at Colosse (*Col. 4:7-8*) and Archippus is the pastor to the church meeting in the house of Philemon (*Col. 4:17, Philemon 1-2*). There is a house church mentioned in Colossians 4:15-16 located in Laodicea. William Barclay suggests this possibility, "This must mean that the letter to Philemon was, in fact written to Laodicea. And, if so, the missing letter to Laodicea, mentioned in Colossians 4:16, is none other than the letter to Philemon. This indeed solves problems."[5] The house church of Colossians 4:15 which meets in Laodicea would be a likely candidate for Philemon's house church except that Nymphas would mind exceedingly much being run out of his own home.

      House churches were the norm of the day, not the exception. There were possibly hundreds of house churches scattered around the region. I recently took a vacation week and traveled to South Korea. I visited a friend my wife and I have there who pastors a church meeting in his apartment home. This was a delightful congregation

---

[5]   William Barclay, *The Letters to Timothy, Titus, and Philemon* (Louisville, KY: Westminster John Knox Press, 2003), 308.

of about 20 faithful Christians. As I looked out at night over the small city of Jeon-Ju where my friend lives, I could see hundreds of red, neon crosses lighting up the sky. I asked my friend what that meant and he told me that most times each house church puts up a cross outside their window from the apartment where they meet. He also went to explain that South Korea is the number two sender of Christian missionaries worldwide, second only to the United States but moving up fast. He stated that South Korean churches don't invest, as a rule, in central buildings for church meetings but rather take the money they raise in their church and use up to 90% of it for mission work. We don't have any literary clues as to where the Philemon mission might be located, but considering the mountainous terrain of the area and the pockets of people that could gather from one valley to another, anything is possible.

Onesimus, Slave or Son?

When I first proposed to do a major project on the letter to Philemon, it was my intent to study this book from the traditional viewpoint of Paul making intercession for a runaway slave named Onesimus. I had glimpsed within Philemon both a message of restoration and ultimately of freedom. The supporting materials that I have read all start out in this same manner. The scenario, always taken at face value and never seriously questioned, is that Onesimus is a slave that stole money from his master Philemon. Thereafter, he found his way to Rome and to the feet of Paul. Once in Paul's influence, he found the Lord and was saved. Paul was sending Onesimus back to Philemon with a letter promoting both restoration and love. It has even been speculated that Paul intended Philemon to send Onesimus back to him to continue his service to Paul while in chains. This scenario might be true, absolutely true, without any mixture of error—might be. Once in the study, however, I began to see other things at work. I began to see the love and intimacy with which Philemon was encouraged to receive again this "slave." I began to see that this departure had ruptured not only a personal relationship but also effected the church κοινονια or fellowship. This letter is addressed not only to Philemon but to a whole congregation. There is no doubt that this work is a legitimate Pastoral Epistle for this reason alone. Questions started to come, and deeper research was conducted into the possibilities.

"Possibilities" is a huge word in this letter to Philemon. The entire book is only 25 verses long with names of people not mentioned in many other places. Some names are never mentioned anywhere else. Almost everything that can be known about the book is contained within the book itself. From verse 16 we get the entire story that Onesimus was a slave, once we assume that δουλοσ is the literal designation for Onesimus. From verse 18 we get the story line that he stole money from Philemon, once we drop the first part of the verse and assume the condition as the reality. We allow ourselves to be indoctrinated and not to think about the deeper meaning of this letter.

Theory is not necessarily fact. It is unfair to assume too much about the characters in this letter. I know that principle goes both ways. However, I am willing to offer a new scenario based on scripture and in line with the emotional tenor of this letter. Onesimus was either a slave as most of the universe has assumed, or a brother to Philemon as the literal translation of verse 16(b) assumes, or a son as I suppose only I assume. Some preachers and scholars like Ray C. Stedman, author and pastor at Peninsula Bible Church, have offered up the literal translation within verse 16 that allows this conjecture, "I think it's quite evident from this verse that Onesimus was Philemon's brother, his literal blood brother."[6] Paul uses the term *adelphos* figuratively in every use. He calls Timothy and Philemon "brothers" in the same letter (*vss. 1 and 7*). Furthermore, I don't find it evident that a brother can actually run away from home, unless the brother was a minor. We don't call brothers runaways if they pack up and move, and they don't need letters of recommendation if they return to the family unit. When my older brother left the house, my

---

[6] Ray C. Stedman "Philemon: A Brother Restored," *Adventuring through the Bible* 258, Message Number 58 (March 1968): 2, http://www.blbi.org/library/pdf/24/24_19.pdf

main concern was getting his room and his golf clubs. If not slave or brother, that leaves only son as the reasonable explanation for words of intense emotion like $αγαπε$ love, $σπλάγχνα$ heart (bowels), $προσλαβοῦ$ receive, and the personal appeal in verse 18 to forgive any trespass that Onesimus might have committed.

I met a professor at the seminary I attended in the early 80's. He was a fire-brand sort of person who liked waging "crusades of truth" throughout his life. He was a prolific author and wonderful thinker. I came to meet him as I was doing a research paper on the "Eternal Security of the Believer" for a class assignment, and I wanted to interview this professor for my paper. He had recently lost his position with the seminary because he had just published a book that took a view not in line with traditional Baptist thought. He had stated to me during my time with him that he had "won" other theological wars in the past, and he was going to "win" this one, too. I will take a view throughout this paper that Onesimus was Philemon's son. I believe there is significant substance to this belief. However, I realize unlike that professor that I fly in the face of two millennia of tradition, and I won't "win" this battle. I will, however, continue to present my views.

Allow me to offer some arguments against the traditional view of Philemon as a *doulos*. Onesimus is called "slave" only in Philemon 16. In other verses he is identified as "a faithful and beloved brother" (*Colossians 4:9*), son of Paul (*Philemon 10*), Paul's own "bowels" (*Philemon 12*), a "brother beloved" (*Philemon 16*), and a "partner" (*Philemon 17*). Surely the designations for something other than "slave" outnumber the one word used twice in verse 16. The word *doulas* is used over 100 times in the New Testament. Of the 29 times Paul uses the word, only 11 of those times is it used in the literal sense of a bondsman. Paul sees all people, including himself, as being a slave of the Lord Jesus Christ when called to Christian service. For him to use the word in Onesimus's situation, he was communicating to Philemon not to see Onesimus simply as a tool for Paul's purposes, but something more familial.

Paul was a scholar in the best of traditions. Certainly he would know of the exact Mosaic Law concerning what to do with a runaway slave. In Deuteronomy 23:15-16 we read, "Thou shalt not deliver unto his master the servant which is escaped from his master unto thee: He shall dwell with thee, even among you, in that place which he shall choose in one of thy gates, where it liketh him best: thou shalt not oppress him." It would be highly unlikely that Paul would go directly against a Mosaic law without so much as an acknowledgement of it to Philemon. Even if he were to turn away from Mosaic Law, Roman law would decree that Paul would be punished for harboring a runaway slave. His quick release from his first Roman incarceration he so earnestly desired would have been at least postponed as more time would be added in the best of dispositions. I don't see Paul breaking a law of God or of man in this situation.

In 1 Timothy 6:1-2, Paul admonishes the *douloi*, slaves under their masters, to provide faithful service. Within this passage, as in his other passages concerning slavery, Paul does not offer any consideration of the emotional well-being of those slaves. Paul gives instruction for the slave of the Christian master to see their master as "beloved" and to work all the more earnestly for that master. In contrast, there is no admonition for the master to love the slave, but only to be fair. Slavery was seen to be a fact of life. In our free society, that seems harsh and cruel. However, there seems to be no situation where Paul seeks to encourage the master to free the slave, Christian servant or not. In 1 Corinthians 7:20, Paul gives instructions to the slaves by saying, "Let every man abide in the same calling wherein he was called." In Philemon, however, we read words of reconciliation, acceptance, love, forgiveness, and freedom. If Onesimus had truly been a slave, then the consistent message from Paul would be addressed to Onesimus and not to Philemon. That message would be for Onesimus to treat Philemon with humility, and to work even harder knowing that he is working for a brother in Christ. Philemon would not have been asked to see Onesimus in any other station in life other than slave, except to simply acknowledge that Onesimus was now a fellow-Christian, and please don't beat him when he returns. This is not the message or tone of the letter to Philemon.

Paul is instructing Philemon to see Onesimus not as "son" in verse 16 because by virtue of Onesimus's conversion he is a "son" of God and therefore spiritual brother to Philemon. Galatians 4:7 states, "Wherefore thou art no more a servant, but a son; and if a son, then an heir of God through Christ." Paul can call Onesimus a son because Paul sees through his work in the ministry, and Onesimus's new life, that Onesimus is a spiritual "son" to the gospel done through him. Onesimus can't be son to God and to Philemon with this new life. Philemon was at one time furious with his "worthless" child (*vs. 11*), but now is being asked to receive him not as a slave, but as a beloved brother in Christ. Onesimus is Philemon's physical son who has run away from the family, and is now being sent back in accordance with the ministry of reconciliation. Luke was the constant companion of Paul. I can see Luke with Paul as Paul writes Philemon. He is sitting with an aware look on his face as Paul tells him of Onesimus and Philemon's life altering situation. Luke is saying to himself, "I know I have heard this before." This is the same story contained in Luke 15:11-32 that we know today as the Prodigal Son.

If conjecture and tradition are the only things going for us in Philemon, which I don't automatically think is the case in every discussion about this letter, then let me at least offer my viewpoint. I have substantial reasons for promoting a view outside the norm. First, we can begin to think and not to be merely indoctrinated. Secondly, we can take seriously all of the inerrant words of Scripture contained in this letter, rightly dividing the word between literal and figurative phrases. Thirdly, the letter is not an accidental occupant of the canon; it is applied ethic and gospel. Finally, with a different viewpoint that Onesimus is the son of Philemon, this letter can come alive again in our churches as parents apply the truths contained within this letter to the situations with their children.

I. GREETING: Vss. 1-3

Paul, a prisoner of Jesus Christ, and Timothy our brother, unto Philemon our dearly beloved, and fellowlabourer, and to our beloved Apphia, and Archippus our fellowsoldier, and to the church in thy house: Grace to you, and peace, from God our Father and the Lord Jesus Christ.

a. Paul, a prisoner

Phm 1 Παῦλοσ δέσμιος Χριστοῦ Ἰησοῦ, καὶ Τιμόθεος ὁ ἀδελφὸς, Φιλήμονι τῷ ἀγαπητῷ καὶ συνεργή ᾧμῶν.

Paul identifies himself in the address line of his New Testament books as a "servant" three times, with no designation in the two letters to the Thessalonians, and an "apostle" seven times, but never before in his introduction as a *δέσμιος*, prisoner. **See Appendix B.** This designation is not only instructive of the circumstances in which he finds himself in Rome, but also establishes his humble place in the ministry before the Lord. At no place in any of the total six places he calls himself a prisoner does he says it was because of any human legal judgment, but rather he is a prisoner of Jesus Christ *(Rom 16:7, Eph. 3:1, Eph. 4:1, 2 Tim. 1:8, Phm. 1, Phm 9)*. Christ is the One who has captivated his life and purpose. Caesar may have been a person who confined Paul in an earthly cell for his preaching of the gospel, but Paul knew that Christ has complete control over his earthly life and spiritual soul. Caesar will take his head but Christ already has his eternal life.

b. Philemon

This letter is primarily addressed to Philemon. It is amazing that this letter was not written to the pastor of the church. Philemon was the eye of the storm of any problems within the church. Philemon is addressed as a loved person by Paul, and a fellow-laborer of Paul and Timothy. It is interesting to note the difference in identification that Paul gives to Timothy and Philemon at this early point. In this letter,

Paul calls Timothy a brother. Paul calls Philemon a loved one. In the other Pastoral Epistles (*1 and 2 Timothy, Titus*) where the letters are addressed to specific people, Paul calls both Timothy and Titus "sons" to designate their status as direct spiritual offspring of the ministry of Paul. Later in this book to Philemon, Paul will use this term to talk about Onesimus.

Paul never calls Philemon his son even though there is a reference in verse 19 that Philemon might have come to know the Lord through Paul's evangelistic ministry. "Son" is used by Paul in very intimate passages. This seems to suggest that Paul either doesn't have a close intimate relationship with Philemon, or he is setting up a position taken within the letter as if he were a subordinate to Philemon. This subordinate position will be used to ask for Onesimus's restoration, as if Paul had his hand out begging for a bit of charity from a benefactor. Philemon was a wealthy and powerful man; therefore he was probably more comfortable when requests were made to him from people with their hands outstretched. It is not really the true spiritual position of the men, but it will be presented by Paul like this for specific reasons as we will see in the course of the exposition.

c. Timothy

The conclusion to the book of Acts talks about Paul's first imprisonment. It does not mention Timothy being in Rome, from where this letter was written. Acts 20 indicates that Timothy may have traveled with Paul as far as Ephesus, but remained there where he became the pastor of that church. However, Acts 28:30 states, "And Paul dwelt two whole years in his own hired house, and received all that came in unto him." Part of that "all" may have easily been Timothy. It appears that Timothy was with Paul in Rome at the time of Philemon being written. This view is also supported in the writing of a companion letter known as the letter to the Colossians.

d. The house-church

Phm 2 καὶ Ἀπφίᾳ τῇ ἀγαπητῇ, καὶ Ἀρχίππῳ τῷ συστρατιώτῃ ἡμῶν, καὶ τῇ κατ'οἶκόν σου ἐκκλησίᾳ

1. Apphia

Apphia is the only woman mentioned in connection with this letter. She is known here as "the beloved." Most scholarship recognizes her as the wife of Philemon. As this is a house church, this assumption is probably the best. The other possibilities are that she is (1) Philemon's sister, (2) Philemon's daughter, (3) Archippus's wife (4) Archippus's daughter, (5) or a strong woman of the church on her own. As this is the only time and context that Apphia is mentioned we have no other context to make a firm decision. This pattern of recognition of husband and wife was acceptable in the New Testament. Ananias and his wife Sapphira in Acts 5:1 are a negative example of Christian life and stewardship. Aquila and his wife Priscilla in Acts 18:2 are a positive example of church growth and faithful support to ministers.

It is amazing that people in our churches today go unrecognized by us. They labor, pray, show faithful stewardship, but they remain in the background. Many people of dynamic faith and fidelity don't want the spotlight cast on them. Think for a minute how many great Biblical Christian examples of the faith are never mentioned because the work they do is behind the scenes, never to be acknowledged in any context. Think how decrepit the church would be today if these same people were not active in the Christian work.

2. *Archippus*

In the companion letter to the Colossians, neither Philemon nor Apphia are mentioned. However, Archippus is mentioned. He is to be instructed by the church in Colosse, "Take heed to the ministry which thou hast received in the Lord, that thou fulfill it." (*Col 4:17*). In Philemon, Archippus is identified by Paul as a fellow-soldier. John Phillips says about Archippus, "He was to regard his ministry as a vessel into which he was to pour all of his life, talents, energy, and power. Here, however, the reference to Archippus is one of warm commendation. He was standing to his post of duty like a valiant soldier, one of Paul's fellow soldiers."[7]

"Fellow-soldier" is a designation used only one other time by Paul. That designation was given to Epaphroditus in Philippians 2:25. While it seems in that reference to be a title equal with "fellow-laborer," here it carries a militaristic connotation not brought forward in other places in the letter of Philemon. Since Archippus was a minister as referenced in the letter to the Colossians, the pastoral function is implied. Therefore, Archippus was the pastor of the church meeting in the house of Philemon. Some have suggested that Epaphroditus was the pastor of the house-church in the letter to Philemon. But that theory doesn't seem to reconcile easily with the statement at the end of Philemon (*vs. 23*) that the church is to welcome Epaphroditus at a later time with other travelers spoken of by Paul.

This letter is sent to a house-church. While most of the pronouns used in this book are singular to address Philemon specifically, there are a few occasions in this letter where the pronouns are plural to address the church. While the book of Philemon is personal in nature, the words are used in a way that suggests Paul means for Philemon to

---

[7] John Phillips, *Exploring Colossians and Philemon*, (Grand Rapids: Kregel, 2002), 240.

be accountable to the church. He is telling Philemon that his actions concerning Onesimus are a church matter, and not just a personal decision on his part. The separation of Onesimus from the family unit has caused repercussions that rocked the church's fellowship. Sides were taken, blame was assigned, and fingers were pointed at who different people thought were to be accused for causing this schism. Slave or son, Onesimus's decision to leave the house was felt by the whole church and needed to be addressed by the whole church.

e. Paul loves the church

Phm 3 χάρις ὑμῖν καὶ εἰρήνη ἀπὸ Θεοῦ πατρὸς ἡμῶν καὶ Κυρίου Ἰησοῦ Χριστοῦ.

Grace and peace, the two-fold blessing given to Timothy and Titus in the other pastorals is here being given to the whole church. The second-person pronoun "you" is plural. Paul wants nothing more than the healing of the church. This healing is through the Lord Jesus Christ. The Lordship of Jesus is mentioned right from the start. This designation for Jesus is used six times in this short letter. Each time (*vss. 3, 5, 16, 20 two times, and 25*) he has put it in a close relationship to either Philemon specifically, or the church as a whole. Jesus is Lord over these lives. When that Lordship is recognized, then the relationship between Philemon and Onesimus will be seen as having a good resolution. Ironside helps to identify the purpose of the letter as being a conduit for reconciliation:

> "It is a remarkable thing that so large a part of the New Testament is made up of letters, a form of literature which leaves room for the most simple, homely touches and which stands in vivid contrast to heavy theological treatises. It is as though our God and Father would speak to our hearts in a tender, familiar manner, calculated to win our fullest confidence."[8]

The concept of God the Father is used in this prayer. The πατροσ manifestation of God is unique to Christianity. Jesus taught his disciples the Fatherhood of God in the Lord's Prayer. Here, as Phillips points out, "Paul underlines the great, revolutionary concept of Christianity—God is the Father of all of those who believe. God was *Paul's* Father, He was *Philemon's* Father, and He was the Father now of *Onesimus*."[9] Paul's attention to this concept allows Philemon to see our Father's love as He offers to His children both grace and peace. Philemon is to offer Onesimus both grace and peace being his earthly father.

---

[8] (Ironside 2008, 178)
[9] (Phillips 2002, 242)

II. Prayers for Philemon vss. 4-6

I Thank my God, making mention of thee always in my prayers, hearing of thy love and faith, which thou hast toward the Lord Jesus, and toward all saints; that the communication of thy faith may become effectual by the acknowledging of every good thing which is in you in Christ Jesus.

a. Paul is Thankful

Phm 4 Εὐχαριστῶ τῷ Θεῷ μου, πάντοτε μνείαν σου ποιούμενος ἐπὶ τῶν προσευχῶν μου,

Paul changes from the second-person plural pronoun to the singular "you" at this point. He is now addressing Philemon specifically; this is still a church matter, but Philemon becomes the focus of the plea to reconcile with Onesimus. Paul begins with expressing positive feelings toward Philemon. He wants to reassure Philemon of his love and respect on a very personal level. There is a lot of ground to cover, but Paul begins with a smile in his voice. He tells Philemon that he is remembered before God with thanksgiving. It is remarkable in this letter that no blame is ever assigned to either Philemon or Onesimus for the latter's departure. Set in the backdrop of a matter that was undoubtedly affecting the church fellowship, this posture goes against the grain of most people. In most of the conflicts that I have seen within different church fellowships, the pointing fingers have been used more often than the listening ears.

John MacArthur writes, "Paul describes the spiritual character of one who forgives in verses 4-7. Such a person has a concern for the Lord, a concern for people, a concern for fellowship, a concern for knowledge, a concern for glory, and a concern to be a blessing."[10] Paul is going to use the power of love to resolve this issue. He will also voice reconciliation in his prayers before God. He is going to remind Philemon that God loves him, and that he has always had a powerful purpose in the family of faith that cannot be sacrificed for any "righteous indignation" that he may feel. When Onesimus is standing in the midst of the congregation with head bowed, ready to hear the consequences of his abandonment of the family, he will have put his fate in the hands of God Who is mutually revered by all. Philemon at that point will be reminded that his actions affect everyone in the church.

b. Paul points to the Builder's Tools

Phm 5 ἀκούων σου τὴν ἀγάπην, καὶ τὴν πίστιν ἣν ἔχεις πρὸς τὸν Κύριον Ἰησοῦν καὶ εἰς πάντας τοὺς ἁγίους,

---

[10] John MacArthur, *Colossians and Philemon*, (Chicago, Moody Publishers: 1992), 209.

This verse starts with love and faith. These two combined attributes of the Christian form the most powerful tools within the Christian community. Love is the only everlasting thing, and faith is the only way to please God. Paul is telling Philemon that he is not alone in his struggles for guidance. Paul assures him that he has a reputation for Godliness. That reputation is one of being a builder of men, and not a destroyer. There is no better way to begin to convey reconciliation than to uplift the people of faith who have interpersonal crisis. The source of these key attributes is the Lord Jesus Christ.

c. Paul shows there is Power in the Church

Phm 6 ὅπως ἡ κοινωνία τῆς πίστεώς σου ἐνεργὴς γένηται ἐν ἐπιγνώσει παντὸς ἀγαθοῦ τοῦ ἐν ὑμῖν ε5ς Χριστὸν Ἰησοῦν.

The word used for "communication" in the KJV is *Koinonia*. Barclay identifies three possible ways to translate this word:

> "(1) *Koinonia* can mean *a sharing in*; it can, for instance, mean partnership in a business. So this may mean *your share in the Christian faith*; and it might be a prayer that the faith in which Philemon and Paul share may lead Philemon deeper and deeper into Christian truth. (2) *Koinonia* can mean *fellowship*; and this may be a prayer that *Christian fellowship*

may lead Philemon ever more deeply into the truth. (3) *Koinonia* can mean the *act of sharing*; in that case, the verse will mean: 'It is my prayer that your way of generously sharing all that you have will lead you more and more deeply in the knowledge of the good things which lead to Christ.'"[11]

The word κοινονια is synonymous with the special relationship shared by the church. It brings with it the idea of a common love among all members. This verse tells us that when we share our goodness within the church, the whole church becomes a more effective witness in the world. These actions are because Christ is the Lord and ruler of conduct of those that share in the faith. Christ directs, and together we share with one another our goodness. Our Spiritual gifts and tools become more effective when used. We sharpen the blades of our axes by their use. By using the plural form for "you", the Holy Spirit is identifying that the goodness is in all the church, and not just one person. Philemon is to join his strength with the church's strength. This will bind his will to the will of the church. Then the church can become the most powerful tool for changing the world as we know it.

---

[11] (Barclay 2003, 314-315)

When I was a child, I used to watch some ridiculous programs for children. One of those shows was Power Rangers. On that show, each character was a different power color—Red Ranger, Blue Ranger, Green Ranger, etc. Each Ranger had a power all his own, but often could be defeated separately by whatever the Big Bad was that week. When the Rangers joined together they formed a Super-Ranger that inevitably won the battle. Even the separate action figures sold in the stores could fit together to form the hero. Now, if the world gets the idea right that together things are stronger than being separate, how come so many church members still just want to come to church and worship God, oblivious of their partners in *Koinonia*? Philemon was not allowed to come to church solely for his relationship to God. He had to take care of his interpersonal relationships, too.

III. For Love's Sake vss. 7-9

For we have great joy and consolation in thy love, because the bowels of the saints are refreshed by thee, brother. Wherefore, though I might be much bold in Christ to enjoin thee that which is convenient, Yet for love's sake I rather beseech thee, being such a one as Paul the aged, and now also a prisoner of Jesus Christ.

a. The Foundation to all Reconciliation is Love.

Phm 7 χάριν γὰρ ἔχομεν πολλὴν καὶ παράκλησιν ἐπὶ τῇ ἀγάπῃ σου, ὅτι τὰ σπλ5γχνα τῶν ἁγίων ἀναπέπαυται διὰ σοῦ, ἀδελφέ.

Properly translated *σπλάγχνα* means "bowels." Literally, this phrase carries a meaning to "soothe the bowels of the saints." Emotions were once seen to reside in the pit of the stomach. We even affirm today when we are disgusted that we are, "Sick to our stomachs!" Since Paul is not advocating an enema in this passage, it is important to redefine the terms in ways we better understand. Therefore the more common understanding of the seat of emotions is the heart. This passage therefore means to "refresh the hearts of the saints." Love is mentioned in this short letter six times. Love is the key and theme in any good relationship within the fellowship of Christ. Paul is addressing specifically Philemon at this time. He is assuring him that because of his love, others in the family are strengthened in their devotion to the Lord. If we love the head of the body, then we must also learn to love the body that is from the neck down, too.

This love spoken of by Paul in this verse is the all-important *agape* love of selflessness. It is the love that puts the needs of others ahead of our own. It is the love that Christ has for the church and the world. It is the highest expression of giving and of service known.

By reminding Philemon of his reputation for this type of love, Paul is already assuring him that what is going to be asked of him is not only possible and reasonable, but also essential and well within his power. All Christian conduct has to be rooted in love, not obligation. All Christian behavior has a direct effect upon the whole body of Christ, and not just a few choice people. By reminding Philemon that he is a Christian brother, Paul is highlighting this obligation for decisions to be based on the needs of others, and not his own selfish interests.

Being refreshed carries with it the idea of being rejuvenated. Christ is the spring of living waters. We can be the people that carry that cool water on a hot day to those who thirst. The Christian message is carried by individuals who have a pure doctrine of loving God and loving their neighbors. This letter does not have a reputation of having a great doctrinal statement. However, it needs to be read with the understanding that it applies the greatest doctrine taught in the Bible. The lessons taught about love for one another are in these passages with a human face.

b. Paul could be Bold

Phm 8 Διὸ πολλ5ν ἐν Χριστῷ παρρησίαν ἔχων ἐπιτάσσειν σοι τὸ ἀνῆκον,

Any boldness that Paul may have in his life, he attributes to Christ. This word, παρρησίαν, is used thirty-one times in the New

Testament. In the context that Paul uses this word, it means that in word or deed he feels confident and open about what he can say. Paul has the apostolic authority and standing within the Christian community to be able to order up things; he sent people places, settled disputes, excommunicated the teachers of false doctrine, and helped ordain the ministers. In the other pastorals, he has not been timid about announcing his authority. In this letter, he does not ever call himself by the word "apostle." The ability to do something is not as important as the need to do something else. As preachers we can pound pulpits and get red in the face over all manner of sin in our church. Sometimes, though, the better road is to be calm and tactful with clear teaching. The proper decision as to which way to present our case is decided by what shows the most love.

Paul points out that any order he could give to Philemon concerning Onesimus would be reasonable, or fitting, for Philemon to carry out. It might make pure sense for Paul to simply tell Philemon what he should do. But would telling him serve the interests of love? Paul doesn't say that it would. He wants Philemon to pay attention to something important to be revealed. It makes the tone of humility Paul is to use all the more potent to the hearer.

c. To Build is not always to use a Hammer

Phm 9 διὰ τὴν ἀγάπην μᾶλλον παρακαλῶ, τοιοῦτος ὢν ὡς Παῦλος πρεσβύτης, νυνὶ δὲ καὶ δέσμιος Ἰησοῦ Χριστοῦ.

There is it again, *agape* love; the reason for everything in this letter. If true reconciliation is to occur, it will because of abundant love. MacArthur says this about the principle of love being used here:

> "Although it is the theme of the letter to Philemon, the word *forgiveness* does not appear in the book. Neither does the articulation of any doctrinal principles that would provide the theological foundation for forgiveness. Paul does not appeal to law or principle but to love (vs. 9). He could do that since he knew Philemon to be a godly, spiritually mature man whose heart was right with God."[12]

Paul had the authority to command Philemon. However, Paul knew that for the needs of the church to be served, the applied law of love must be exercised. Paul recognized Philemon's right to choose the path he would take. This also meant that Paul had opened the door for Philemon to exact terrible revenge upon Onesimus because of the pain and humiliation that Onesimus had undoubtedly caused him.

---

[12] (MacArthur 1992, 218)

Others in the church probably blamed Philemon for being too hard on Onesimus to make him want to leave. Philemon had lost respect in the community because of it. Maybe others were critical of Philemon for not being able to rule his household better. Now, with Onesimus in the midst of the congregation, it was Philemon's opportunity to get even and to get some measure of respect back. But that would mean power and not love would be served. Paul knew that for any positive thing to be built in the congregation, it would have to come from love. Reconciliation is not the reminder of who is in control, rather it is the exercise of the love that God gives to us as shown to the world by the Lord Jesus Christ.

Humility is the tone of this letter to Philemon. In the two other times the exact term πρεσβύτης is used (*Luke 1:18, Titus 2:2*), it is used to reference the chronological age of a man. This is not Paul saying he is an elder within the church; it is Paul painting a picture for Philemon of a 60 year old man. While that isn't old by our standards, Paul had to endure incredible hardships throughout his ministry that surely wore on him beyond his years. As they say, "It's not the age, it's the mileage." Paul had a lot of miles on him with many more to go. In communicating to Philemon, he might have even let his voice thin and cough a little bit while proof reading this letter before it was sent out. These words are not shouted. They are whispered. In the whispering, they are heard all the more.

IV. Paul Makes His Request Known vss. 10-14

I beseech thee for my son Onesimus, whom I have begotten in my bonds: Which in time past was to thee unprofitable, but now profitable to thee and to me: Whom I have sent again: thou therefore receive him, that is, mine own bowels: Whom I would have retained with me, that in thy stead he might have ministered unto me in the bonds of the gospel: But without thy mind would I do nothing; that thy benefit should not be as it were of necessity, but willingly.

a. Onesimus

Phm 10 Παρακαλῶ σε περὶ τοῦ ἐμοῦ τέκνου, ὃν ἐγέννησα 5ν τοῖς δεσμοῖς μου, Ὀνήσιμον,

Paul continues his letter in the voice of the aged prisoner. He is not commanding, he is asking. The word used for this asking is the same word for *Paraclete,* the Comforter, or the Holy Spirit. This is a soft voice that Paul is using. He wants to encourage Philemon to listen to his desires. He wants to teach Philemon a lesson in love by using love. He wants to give comfort to the church by having a matter resolved in love, that the ministry of reconciliation can be shown in the church.

Within this request Paul is asking either "on behalf of" Onesimus, or he is asking "for" Onesimus. The word περὶ can be translated either way with the meaning of the verse changing dramatically. If the translation means that Paul is asking on behalf of Onesimus, then Paul is asking that Philemon reconcile with Onesimus. If Paul is asking for Onesimus, then it would be, as George A. Buttrick points out in his exposition of Philemon, "Certainly... Paul wants (*Onesimus*) to be returned to him."[13] Onesimus has proven himself to be a faithful companion. While Paul could have used his apostolic authority to command that Onesimus be returned to him, he chose to give Philemon the opportunity to prove his usefulness to Paul. I feel that Paul intentionally used a word that may be construed either way. Paul was saying to Philemon both things. Obviously he wanted reconciliation to occur. Furthermore, it was his desire that Onesimus continue in the service of the Lord. If Philemon consents, then not only does Paul get a fellow-laborer but also the Lord gets a new servant. Paul would surely like to use Onesimus to help him prepare for any future trip he might take to Philemon's church.

For the first time in the letter he mentions the cause of Philemon's pain by name, Onesimus. I know that many commentators make a huge deal about the name meaning "Profitable." They sometimes talk about it as if it were a divinely inspired name to give more authority to the letter of Philemon than it may properly deserve.

---

[13] *The Interpreter's Bible*, s.v. "Exposition of Philemon."

I don't take much stock in interpreting names in the Bible unless they are names given to people later in life to describe something of their personalities. Simon Peter is a great case in point; his special name given to him by Jesus means "Rock" in Matthew 16:18. My first name is Philip, and it means "lover of horses." Truthfully, I don't care too much for the animals. They intimidate me. While Onesimus means "Profitable," it is hard to see that if his name was Fred the letter to Philemon would be any less valuable to the Christian church today.

In Colossians 4:9, Onesimus is called a faithful and beloved brother. Philemon 10 calls Onesimus a son. This designation is the result of Onesimus coming to know the Lord under Paul's direct influence. The occasion of this conversion was while Paul was a prisoner the first time in Rome. Onesimus could identify with Paul's imprisonment, as Onesimus felt like he was a prisoner to his actions and misdeeds. Slave or son, while Onesimus was in flight from the household of Philemon, Philemon owned him totally. Every dream and every thought was on his dire situation. He could not help but look over his shoulder every waking day. Philemon had rented space in Onesimus's head the size of a mansion. What he thought was freedom he now could see by experience was worse than any form of slavery he could imagine because it affected his soul. During this time that the relationship with Philemon was broken, Onesimus would always be ruled by fear and failure. In meeting Paul, Onesimus saw a person with visible chains where his were invisible. In hearing Paul talk victoriously about Jesus, Onesimus heard about the one Person who could make him free, and free indeed. The decision to return to Philemon after his conversion was inevitable. Only in returning could his freedom be secured in this life as well as the next.

b. Being Profitable

Phm 11 τὸν ποτέ σοι ἄχρηστον, νυνὶ δέ σοι καὶ ἐμοὶ εὔχρηστον,

Being of use in the Lord's work apparently is not an option. *Chrestos* is the word for profitable in this verse. The root word here hangs like the fulcrum of a child's teeter-totter. If the bigger child gets on the left side, then the left side hits the ground first. *Chrestos* is being tipped by its prefixes. First, Onesimus was ἄχρηστον or worthless. He had been seen by Philemon as a liability and a hindrance. This is what Philemon thought of Onesimus, first in his position in the household when he was there, but now in his absence that he is gone. Many times Philemon uttered the word "worthless" to describe Onesimus. Slave or son, no one likes to hear those words and would gladly see running away as an alternative. By saying εὔχρηστον Paul declares that a transformation has occurred in Onesimus's life. Onesimus had become precious to him. The quality of his character, not just his abilities, had changed. Everyone in the family of God has powers and abilities. When reconciliation occurs, it is because these beneficial traits of people are mutually recognized. No one is beyond redemption. The church has the ministry of reconciliation because Christ is in the hearts of those of good faith. People may stumble, but then Christ can lift them back up.

By the words of this scripture, Paul is pointing out clearly that the difference in Onesimus's life is the change brought by a newly found relationship with Jesus Christ. Paul has recognized certain attributes that Onesimus has that makes him useful in God's work. Christian leaders should be alert to the abilities of others in their membership. When we need to seek reconciliation in our conflicts, we need to see the benefits of redeeming the relationship. We see the benefits best when we see the unique talents and abilities spiritually within other people. Onesimus has caused a crisis in the church; first by departing, and now by showing back up. The foundation for resolution has been carefully laid out. The themes of the Lordship of Christ have been proclaimed. Love must be served, not power. Philemon has a choice to make. The health of the church hangs in the balance of his decision.

c. Refresh my heart, Receive him.

Phm 12 ὃν ἀνέπεμψα σὺ δὲ αὐτὸν, τουτ ἐστι τὰ ἐμὰ σπλάγχνα, προσλαβοῦ,

In verse 7, Paul stated in his prayer of thanksgiving that Philemon had the reputation for refreshing the hearts of the saints. Here, Paul is asking no less of Philemon for himself. By setting the tone early on, Paul is now putting Philemon in somewhat of a bind. If he were to pass a harsh judgment upon Onesimus not only would he be impacting the church in a negative way, he would be inflicting more suffering upon Paul during his imprisonment. Barclay says this about Paul's plea for reconciliation, "When someone has made a mistake, the way back can be very hard, and God cannot readily forgive anyone who, through self-righteousness or lack of sympathy, makes it harder."[14] Paul is painting Philemon into a corner that will most assuredly result in reconciliation with Onesimus. Slave or son, Onesimus will soon be as free emotionally as he already is spiritually.

The word derived from *Proslambano* is translated "receive him". This word is meant to ask of Philemon not only that he would take Onesimus back, but that he would receive him with the quality of mercy in his heart. My church has a custom after someone comes forward to join our congregation that we "extend to them the right hand of fellowship." It is a good way for everyone to greet the new member and give official recognition that this person is now an equal part of our family. It is more than saying congratulations for

---

[14] (Barclay 2003, 318)

a good decision; it is an affirmation of our love and support. The word used by Paul has the quality of warmth and care. Philemon is being instructed not only to refrain from harming Onesimus, but he is asked to receive him into the fellowship of believers with love. This imagery of ingathering is in sharp contrast to Jesus's words as he wept over Jerusalem in Luke 13:34:

O Jerusalem, Jerusalem, which killest the prophets, and stonest them that are sent unto thee; how often would I have gathered thy children together, as a hen doth gather her brood under her wings, and ye would not!

d. The Obligation of Service

Phm 13 ὃν ἐγὼ ἐβουλόμην πρὸς ἐμαυτὸν κατέχειν, ἵνα ὑπὲρ σοῦ διακονῇ μοι ἐν τοῖς δεσμοῖς τοῦ εὐαγγελίου

Paul shares his desire that Onesimus could remain with him. In this statement, he is reaffirming to Philemon that Onesimus is a positive benefit to his work, and not the liability that Philemon at one time felt about the "worthless Onesimus". Unspoken in this verse, but obvious by its context is Paul's desire to have Onesimus reconciled to the church and then freely sent back by the church to continue the work with Paul. If Onesimus were to be sent back to Paul freely, then he could hold his head up high. The work of the ministry is to be joyful and fulfilling. When we become reconciled to each other, the whole church is a place of blessings.

Spoken in this verse is an obligation that Paul puts upon Philemon. Paul the aged prisoner shows some teeth to his request. He reminds Philemon that he has a debt of service to Paul in his chains. By having Onesimus serve in his place, Philemon can pay that debt. No one in the church is so isolated that we don't share in each other's service. There are thousands of Christian missionaries serving in places where many of us may not want to visit. Many people today say they would not want to live in Haiti, the poorest place on this side of the planet. Yet, there are hundreds of thousands of souls who live there who need the Lord. It is God's plan to send missionaries to these places. I had the privilege of preaching in a church in Haiti where the support beams were tree limbs and the walls were bed sheets. The people walked for a couple of miles or more to bring their families to this church with gravel flooring. The music was lively and the Spirit of the Lord was there. Today, we help support missionaries with a portion of our church funds who continue the work there, and around the world. Many good and regular church members have never seen their own passport photo. We serve side-by-side with those around the world when we pray and support the missionaries on the field. This was Philemon's obligation to Paul.

Paul reminded Philemon that it was his job to work beside him. Philemon would have to view Onesimus in a different way now. He would have to begin to see Onesimus as a down-payment on eternal service to be rendered. With Onesimus now standing in the midst of the congregation, Philemon could squander his opportunity to make good on that debt, or pay on that debt by sending Onesimus back to Paul with his blessing, and the blessing of the church. The ministry of reconciliation now shows a purpose beyond just feeling good about one another and resolving conflicts. It empowers people to be vital instruments in the service of our Lord.

It is interesting to note that Paul's prison is not made with brick and mortar. It is the imprisonment of the gospel. I am sure that he is not saying that the ministry is a terrible thing, but rather he is saying that he is captive to it and would not be released from its goodness and its joy. The gospel is all encompassing. It is not just a weekend job, or an optional hobby. When a person receives the Call from the Lord, it is for life and everything within life that makes it worth living.

e. It is Better to Want than to Need

Phm 14 χωρὶς δὲ τῆς σῆς γνώμης οὐδὲν ἠθέλησα ποιῆσαι, ἵνα μὴ ὡς κατὰ ἀνάγκην τὸ ἀγαθόν σου ᾖ, ἀλλὰ κατὰ ἑκούσιον.

Verses 8 and 9 stated that Paul knew he had the authority to command Philemon to be reconciled to Onesimus; however, he chose to encourage him toward this reconciliation. Paul realizes that while he might have the apostolic authority to retain Onesimus by making a unilateral decision, he wanted to gain Philemon's agreement. This is another point to make against the traditional designation of "slave" as it applies to Onesimus. On the one hand, the Mosaic Law would instruct Paul not to return Onesimus to Philemon. On the other hand, Roman law would punish Paul for keeping him. While both laws contradict each other, Paul would have to make a decision within the influence of either Mosaic or Roman law. In any case, Paul would not see it as simple as his option to keep Onesimus, or gently ask for Philemon's opinion on the matter. If Paul were to outright violate either law, he would have made literary reference to some principle to follow. Instead he simply says, "I wanted (*not needed*) to keep him with me, but I wasn't going to without your (*not Roman law's*) input."

The purpose of asking graciously becomes clear with Paul's use of ἀγαθόν. Paul is stating that he is leaving it up to Philemon to choose what happens so that Philemon can receive the blessing. The strong implication is that Philemon will do the right thing and have reconciliation with Onesimus. This is something that Philemon should want to do at this point. "I want to" is a far better thing to say than "I have to." When the church sees Philemon willingly restore Onesimus, they will share in that goodness.

V. There is a Reason to Everything vss. 15-17

For perhaps he therefore departed for a season, that thou shouldest receive him forever; Not now as a servant, but above a servant, a brother beloved, especially to me, but how much more unto thee, both in the flesh and in the Lord? If thou count me therefore a partner, receive him as myself.

a. Time and Times

Phm 15 τάχα γὰρ διὰ τοῦτο ἐχωρίσθη πρὸς ὥραν, ἵνα αἰώνιον αὐτὸν ἀπέχῃς,

I can see at this point in the letter to Philemon, Luke, the beloved physician and constant shadow of Paul, is having a good chuckle in the corner of the room about these verses. In Luke 15:11-32, he recorded a parable spoken by Jesus about a lost son. This son had departed from his father after gaining a small inheritance, money that was not due him at that time because the father was still alive. Once financially independent, the son abandoned the family and set off to greener pastures, only to find out that the pastures were trodden under by pigs. The son, during the time of his exile, "came to himself" in vs. 17 and repented. I can see Luke remembering that great story of the Prodigal Son and inescapably couldn't resist seeing the parallels with this real life story of Onesimus. In fact, if this event had happened prior to Jesus, then the prodigal might have had a real name, Onesimus.

The time that Onesimus had departed was used by the Lord to allow Onesimus to come into contact with Paul, listen to the gospel, and find everlasting life. The passage of time was but a twinkle in the eye of God. Now, here was Onesimus standing in the church before Philemon and the others. Paul reasoned that because Onesimus separated from the family briefly, he could now become a full family member for all of eternity. Paul gives the running away reason and purpose. Philemon and the others had to begin to see that there was a plan God had in store for Onesimus that included his leaving. Philemon could no longer see the "worthless Onesimus" as simply a runaway who caused him grief, because God used those events to redeem another lost soul. Onesimus now stands before the congregation a spiritual man, worthy of an everlasting bond of love given by his brothers and sisters.

"But the father said to his servants, Bring forth the best robe, and put it on him; and put a ring on his hand, and shoes on his feet: And bring hither the fatted calf, and kill it; and let us eat, and be

merry: For this my son was dead, and is alive again: he was lost, and is found; And they began to be merry." Luke 15:22-24

b. Onesimus, once the Slave

Phm 16 οὐκέτι ὡς δοῦλον, ἀλλ᾽ ὑπὲρ δοῦλον, ἀδελφὸν ἀγαπητὸν, μάλιστα ἐμοί, πόσῳ δὲ μᾶλλόν σοι καὶ ἐν σαρκὶ καὶ ἐν Κυρίῳ.

This is the only verse in which we have the word *δοῦλον,* meaning "slave," applied to Onesimus. From this single word used twice in this verse, and in no other place applied to Onesimus, we get the traditional suggestion that Onesimus was a slave that had run away from Philemon. An entire epic saga springs from this one verse. Onesimus is said to have stolen money from Philemon, run away to Rome seeking refuge, finding Paul and being converted, returning to Philemon, and later becoming Bishop of the church in Colosse, ultimately to collect the letters of Paul into a single collection. The only reason that this collection included the letter to Philemon was because Bishop Onesimus had a sentimental attachment to it, or so the story goes. If *δοῦλον* is taken literally as the official designation for Onesimus, then this scenario is entirely possible. If the word *δοῦλον* is figurative, then a new scenario must be built. It is interesting to note that while the word for slave in the first part of the verse is accepted as literal, the word *ἀδελφὸν* in the same verse is interpreted figuratively. I feel both words should be taken from the physical viewpoint as figurative, but from the spiritual viewpoint as absolutely, descriptively literal.

In the final analysis, we really can't say for absolute certainty what Onesimus's role in the household truly was. As I have already pointed out, the similarities between this letter and Luke 15:11-32 are striking. The prodigal thought he was going to have to come back to his father as a slave. A person can literally sell themselves into slavery to repay debts. Paul may have been asking Philemon not to bind Onesimus in this type of debt-servitude as a form of punishment if Onesimus had truly stolen something from Philemon. After all, it was in the next breath that Paul talked about a potential restitution issue. However, there are bigger issues in this verse than any monetary crimes. There is no greater hurt in a man's heart than when a family member rebels and leaves the house. No greater anger is kindled within the father. It often seems the urge to punish far outweighs the need to forgive. In contrast, there is no greater joy than when the wayward son returns to the home in humility seeking reconciliation. The overall tone contained within the letter to Philemon conveys warmth, affection, and deep human emotion. It would be hard to see any of the deepest of these emotions being transferred to a slave, even if that slave were forgiven of running away and theft. Onesimus had been transformed by the power of the cross from a slave to his fears to a beloved brother in the Lord. Paul has gained a son and a brother at the same time, according to his words (*vss. 10 and 16*). If Paul so regarded Onesimus, then the conclusion is that the church must also regard Onesimus as a beloved brother, too. This is to be both "in the flesh and in the Lord," or in the physical as well as spiritual reality. This transformation is because of Christ.

The Stephens Edition of the Textus Receptus of 1550 adds a line after the "Amen" of vs. 25 of Philemon. That additional material identifies Onesimus as the *ouiketo*, House Servant, which is a different form of indentured servant than a δοῦλον. The two types differ in privilege and status within a house. The King James Version does not carry the translation of the Stephens TR at this point. By the time of the Scrivener's Edition of 1881, all of this variant material is omitted.

a. Onesimus, now the partner

Phm 17 εἰ οὖν ἐμὲ ἔχεις κοινωνόν, προσλαβοῦ αὐτὸν ὡς ἐμέ.

In this verse, Paul asks the fellowship to see Onesimus as they would see Paul, himself. Paul is bestowing the same credentials as "partner of the church" to Onesimus. As the church would recognize Paul as a missionary, faithful instructor, and embattled prisoner of the gospel; so now, they are to recognize Onesimus. The word *κοινωνὸν* is used here as it was in verse 6, when Paul was asking for strength from the church's faith and love. The word *προσλαβοῦ* is used here as it was in verse 12, repeating the instructions to the church to receive Onesimus with love because they would receive Paul with love. Charles Ray puts it this way, "This receiving should match Philemon's esteem and regard for the apostle and be done in the same manner he would adopt if his own spiritual father would suddenly appear. This welcome was to be joyous and open and should not in any way be spoiled by recriminations, spite, or malice."[15] Any wrath that Philemon might have had with Onesimus would by now be done away with. The ministry of reconciliation would be complete. The principle of love would be served.

VI. Paul Addresses Consequences vss. 18-20

If he hath wronged thee, or oweth thee aught, put that on mine account; I Paul have written it with mine own hand, I will repay it: albeit I do not say to thee how thou owest unto me even thine own self besides. Yea, brother, let me have joy of thee in the Lord: refresh my bowels in the Lord.

a. Balancing some Books

Phm 18 εἰ δέ τι ἠδίκησέ σε ἢ ὀφείλει, τοῦτο ἐμοὶ ἐλλόγει

---

[15] Charles Ray, The Books of First and Second Timothy, Titus, and Philemon: Goals to Godliness, (Chattanooga, TN, AMG Publishers: 2008), 216.

In the preceding verses, Paul has dealt with the emotional and spiritual issues of reconciliation. He has laid a sturdy foundation in Christ that seems to settle all the issues of a conflict within the body of Christ. There is always, however, the "yes-but" aspect of conflict. What about the physical costs of conflict? How is the church to handle situations where there is real loss financial or otherwise? Paul provides guidance towards that answer. Compare this to his teaching on lawsuits between Christians in I Corinthians 6:1-3:

"Dare any of you, having a matter against another, go to law before the unjust, and not before the saints: Do ye not know that the saints shall judge the world? And if the world shall be judged by you, are ye unworthy to judge the smallest matters? Know ye not that we shall judge angels? How much more things that pertain to this life?"

Paul even goes on to say in verse 7 that it is better to suffer the loss of finances or harm than to submit to a court of law in the jurisdiction of those outside the church.

In this verse, Paul states to Philemon two things and not just one. The first concerns issues not financial in nature. Paul allows Philemon to take stock of any wrongs that Onesimus may have done. I say may have because of the conditional "if" in the verse. This would allow Philemon an opportunity to inventory all of the insults and ridicule he suffered because of Onesimus's departure. Onesimus's running away had a direct reflection upon the prestige of Philemon within the family. Philemon was rich, powerful, and the owner of the house where the church met (*vs. 2*). We can relate to the image of the family as a positive example within the church. Fairly or unfairly, in many people's eyes today a Pastor with a family is seen as more stable and desirable as a Christian example than one who ministers alone. Certainly, to have a family member, and then to lose them will be a scandal within the church; people will take sides, blame will be assigned, and reputations will be tarnished. Philemon was allowed a moment to gather his thoughts on these matters, and count the cost he has suffered.

Secondly, Philemon was allowed by Paul to account for any missing money, if there was any taken. Tradition tells us that when the slave Onesimus ran away he stole from Philemon part of his fortune. He might have seen some of this money as necessary to make any long trip for his escape. He also might have seen this money as due him as compensation for the toil he did on behalf of Philemon. Philemon got rich because of Onesimus's labor. Paul tells Philemon to provide an accurate account of any monies stolen, which might have been substantial. It takes real money to travel far distances, and for extended periods of time. As a comparison, refer back to the Prodigal in Luke's gospel to see if the runaway son wanted a piece of dad's pie. I am the youngest of three children. My dad has often said I will get a third of his assets when he is gone. In reality, I will probably have a third of dad's bills to pay after his funeral. I am not anxious to collect either one.

What Paul then says to Philemon is incredible and universally overlooked. He tells Philemon, not in a whispering voice either, "put those things on my account." It becomes paid in full at that moment. What a statement. Now, here is the really incredible part. Paul would not have such a real financial account. First of all, any "wrongs" might not be able to be quantified with any physical artifact or financial amount. How much is your reputation worth to you? How much are you worth? No one can say. Therefore, the accounting would be impossible. Secondly, when it does come to the financial aspect of this verse, Paul is in prison in Rome. He had been incarcerated for a total of about 4 years at this point. He did not have the ability to work his secular job of making tents for quite some time. According to Acts 28:30, Paul is under what we would call today "House Arrest." The verse states that he is in a house he has to rent for two years. If Paul has any income from generous donors coming to him for his daily sustenance, he would be using it for rent on the house and his basic needs. Any excess funds would be used to expand the gospel. Paul would never divert church money for his own gain even if by doing so it would have meant his freedom (*Acts24:26-27*). Furthermore, Paul would rather make tents than accept financial gain for preaching the gospel. Paul had no extra bank account that he could rely upon as a super-fund for expenditures such as would be required in Philemon's case.

In the days before the full extent of the scandal was known about the Praise the Lord (*PTL*) organization of Jim and Tammy Fay Bakker, Jim Bakker was found to have had an affair with a church secretary in Clearwater, FL. In 1980, he and another man, John Wesley Fletcher, had a sexual encounter with 21 year old Jessica Hahn. Jessica Hahn maintained her silence after her rape by both of these men. Jessica Hahn received $279,000.00 to keep the violation a secret. The scandal only broke in 1987 when the finances of the PTL organization underwent extreme scrutiny due to real-estate fraud that eventually led to Jim Bakker's imprisonment. Jessica Hahn's silence was paid for by the donations of well-meaning people all over the world, thinking they were giving money for Jim Bakker to spread the word of God. What was meant to buy shouting bought only silence. This is an extreme example of what it looks like when ministers and ministries play "hide and seek" with their finances. Paul would never had received a dime for the work of the gospel that he would by any means give to Philemon for Onesimus's sake, even if he had any. Even if he had some measure of personal wealth, he would have seen it as scandalous to operate in such a manner. Ironside offers the proper interpretation of this verse, "The great doctrine of substitution is illustrated by Paul's offer to pay his debt. The truth of acceptance is suggested when Paul intimates that they are to show their regard for him by the way they treat Onesimus. It is a delightful miniature of the evangel."[16]

So what is meant by "put it on my account?" Paul is telling Philemon to see any debts, real or imagined, as being payable by the imprisonment that he is suffering for all the work of the gospel. With every stripe of every whip, Paul is making investment in the lives he will touch with the gospel. With every day being shipwrecked, Paul is offering to the Lord his fortune of life and breath. With every rotation of the axe man's wheel that will one day take the life of this Apostle born out of season, Paul is laying up a treasure in heaven where neither moth nor rust corrupt. By saying, "put it on my account" Paul is telling Philemon, "I am responsible."

b. Balancing the Right Books

Phm 19 ἐγὼ Παῦλος ἔγραψα τῇ ἐμῇ χειρί, ἐγὼ ἀποτίσω ἵνα μὴ λέγω σοι ὅτι καὶ σεαυτόν μοι προσοφείλεις.

Paul wrote the book of Galatians with his own hand, and referenced that action in Galatians 6:11 because of the importance he placed on doctrine. Here in Philemon the reference to Paul's own hand is used for emphasis placed on the matter at hand. Don't be so

---

[16] (Ironside 2008, 182)

hasty to ask for what is due you, when you realize how much you owe another. No one is isolated in the Kingdom's work. Paul emphatically states that any debt is his responsibility. He will surely pay it. I often wonder as I read 2 Timothy 4:8 when Paul is contemplating his death and using the term for his reward as "Crown" that he is not somehow thinking about his role upon the death of Stephen in Acts 7:58; for he cannot speak the word, Crown, without saying the name, Stephen. At that martyrdom, Paul became indebted to Stephen, and Stephen's debts were fully paid. With Paul's execution for the gospel's sake anything owed to Philemon touching the work of the gospel and of Onesimus would be stamped, "paid in full."

Sometime in AD 67, less than a decade after this letter was written to Philemon, Paul will be led out into the light of day; a light that he would have been deprived of for several months in the belly of the Mamertine prison. Aged, weak, and sickly, Paul would be led out by others to a place on the roadside leading to Rome. Luke would be a witness, as would possibly Timothy in his own bonds later to be released after the suicide of Nero. His crime was living the life of a true Christian. The evidence against him was the lives of those he converted, including Timothy, Titus, Onesimus, Philemon, and a host of others. His sentence was death by decapitation. Being a free-born Roman Citizen he could not suffer crucifixion, the fate of the Jewish Apostle Peter. Crazed, diseased, and demon-possessed, Nero would get his pound of flesh, actually approximately 10 pounds –the weight of an average human head–from Paul. But that is all he would get. Heaven got all of the good stuff, body and soul. As Jesus would say some thirty years before, "It is finished." The debt is paid.

The concluding part of this verse highlights this point beyond all speculation. Paul states to Philemon in what is rather a sarcastic tone, "albeit I do not say to thee how thou owest unto me even thine own self besides." Don't miss this point. Paul has just snapped a great verbal trap set for Philemon since the opening words of this letter. The same debt which Philemon might have placed at the feet of Paul in verse 18 is the exact debt that Philemon owes to Paul in verse 19. Paul, the aged prisoner, had been begging for reconciliation from Philemon, ruler of his house and financier of the churches of Colosse. Now, Paul was saying in today's youthful vernacular, "Who's your daddy?"

The disposition of the relationship with Onesimus hung in the balance. Paul was going to make sure that nothing of the flesh or of the spirit was going to stand in the way of love's purpose being served. If Onesimus was a slave, as most have suggested, then this one passage would inevitably have led Philemon to free him on the spot, and make a motion before the church to ordain him a missionary to serve at Paul's side. If Onesimus was a son, then Philemon would have no other reaction (if he were any caring father at all) than to fall in his son's arms and welcome him back to the family with tears of joy. Speculative tradition aside, history does not allow us to know what happened. That's good. I think private moments between father and son should remain private.

For true reconciliation to occur, forgiveness has to happen. People cannot harbor the misdeeds of the past no matter how hurtful or expensive. When couples fight, it often gets nasty; tears are shed, voices are raised, doors are slammed, and worse yet past histories are brought up again and again as if they occurred just moments before. They say, "Forgive and forget." I'm not sure that is possible. I don't think even God can forget if that means erasing events of the past from his consciousness. What I do think happens with God and should happen with man is that we need to stop making another person relive harsh moments as if they were still happening. Our example of perfect forgiveness is in the Cross of Jesus Christ. He paid the price none of us can pay, once and for all.

c. Do the Right Thing

Phm 20 ναὶ, ἀδελφέ, ἐγώ σου ὀνα5μην ἐν Κυρίῳ ἀνάπαυσόν μου τὰ σπλάγχνα ἐν Κυρίῳ

The word ὀναίμην is used only in this verse in the entire New Testament. It comes from another Greek word meaning "name." It seems to carry the idea of being noteworthy in the assistance being given; noteworthy aid and comfort leads to a joyful outcome. Being helped and being joyful are synonymous with this word. The name Onesimus comes from this word, to mean "useful." This verse carries an almost word-for-word repetition of verse 7. Paul calls Philemon by the term brother now twice in this letter. Paul pointed out that Philemon was helpful to the other Christians in the community when he stated that Philemon was able to make the Christians more joyful in their heart. Here, Paul is asking the same thing from Philemon towards himself. Philemon can make a name for himself in the Lord, not by using power but by applying love. Refreshing begins in the Lordship of Jesus Christ. The word for Lord is used twice in verse 20 for emphasis. By invoking another use of the word Lord, Paul is reminding Philemon that, "He must not act out of benevolence to Onesimus or out of pity for Paul. He must act out of direct responsibility to the Lord."[17]

VII. Looking Ahead Together vss. 21-24

Having confidence in thy obedience I wrote unto thee, knowing that thou wilt also do more than I say. But withal prepare me also a lodging: for I trust that through your prayers I shall be given unto you. There salute thee Epaphras, my fellow prisoner in Christ Jesus:

---

[17] (Phillips 2002, 262)

Marcus, Aristarchus, Demas, Lucas, my fellow laborers. The grace of our Lord Jesus Christ be with your spirit. Amen

a. "Having confidence in thy obedience. . ."

Phm 21 πεποιθὼς τῇ ὑπακοῇ σου ἔγραψά σοι, εἰδὼς ὅτι καὶ ὑπὲρ ὃ λέγω ποιήσεις.

The word πεποιθώς is the same word used in 2 Timothy 1:12. It means to be confident of something, and to trust. Paul is confident that the outcome of this conflict between Philemon and Onesimus will be settled in love's favor. In the ministry of reconciliation, it is always good to know that everyone is dealing with people of good will who want to see resolution. Some people just want to complain, cause dissention, and serve selfish pride. Paul has recognized that Philemon really wants to do the right thing, and just needs a bit of encouragement. McGee acknowledges the Christian impulse to do better than good, "It is characteristic of real believers to do more than is requested. Jesus asks us to go the second mile."[18] Paul recognized that Philemon had been refreshing to the saints in the church, and that he genuinely had a type of faith that builds up people. He just needed to know how to use these valuable traits to overcome his own hurt in the situation with Onesimus. Paul had begun the letter with

---

[18] (McGee 1991, 191)

positive things to say about Philemon, and now he is concluding the letter the same way. He is setting the tone of his note about coming to visit to be a positive event instead of a visit of impending doom.

b. Paul's Plans

Phm 22 ἅμα δ5 καὶ ἑτοίμαζέ μοι ξενίαν ἐλπίζω γὰρ ὅτι διὰ τῶν προσευχῶν ὑμῶν χαρισθήσομαι ὑμῖν.

The "more than I say" of verse 21 is here revealed in verse 22. Paul would very much like to visit Colosse. Apparently, he believes that his two year house arrest mentioned in Acts 28 will soon come to a happy end, and he will be allowed to resume his travels unhindered. He has also stated, however, that he really wants to journey to Spain (*Romans 15:24-28*). Apparently not only does Paul want to be ". . .all things to all men that I might by all means save some" (*I Corinthians 9:22*) He also wants to be everywhere at all times in order to visit some.

I don't think Paul ever made it to Spain. It is more probable that once released, he remained in the area of Asia Minor. The writing of the Pastoral letters to Ephesus and Crete seem to bear this out. Time also testifies to this theory as the end of this first imprisonment (AD 62) and the beginning of his second and final imprisonment (AD 66) were only four years. I am convinced that this first Roman imprisonment took a lot out of Paul no matter how loosely the chains were bound. It is easy to see that a man in his 60's, who had some maladies anyway including an unspecified "thorn in the flesh" (*2 Corinthians 12:7*), would need time to recuperate after any confinement. Paul's declared plans to Philemon about coming to the church were for just this reason (*vss. 20-22*). He is not about to start traveling to begin an intense new project in Spain the day after getting out of chains in Rome. With the matters brewing around Ephesus and Crete that caused the writing of the letters of 1 Timothy and Titus, I believe Paul focused on more local issues. A possible trip, then, to Colosse seems much more likely, especially in light of his desire for a time of renewal and the close proximity of Colosse to Ephesus.

In the latter half of this verse, Paul uses the second-person plural forms for "you." This indicates that the focus again is on the church. This letter had been read in public most probably by Archippus, the pastor of the house-church. Philemon was to secure proper lodging for Paul and his companions, and when they arrive it will be because the prayers of the church were answered by God. The word Paul uses that is translated by the King James Version as "I shall be given" is the derivative of *Charizomai*. It is a word that also means to "graciously restore something." Paul is looking to Christ to work through the church to reinvigorate his life and ministry through grace. Grace is the active force in this passage. The need for grace is evident in all of the church's dealings, on behalf of Paul and on behalf of Onesimus. Likewise, MacArthur points out that Paul uses this reference to prayer effectively, "Philemon could hardly pray for God to bring Paul to Colossae if he had not forgiven Onesimus."[19]

c. Epaphras

Phm 23 Ἀσπάζονταί σε Ἐπαφρᾶς ὁ συναιχμάλωτός μου ἐν Χριστῷ Ἰησοῦ,

The church is to welcome Epaphras. He is mentioned with special favor here more than the other men. In Colossians 4:12, he is identified as a "servant of Christ" and a Colossian. Philemon would have known this person well. The other men who were being sent out by Paul occupy a list together in the next verse. Epaphras is identified in the letter to Philemon as a "fellow-prisoner." Paul uses this term only twice before. In Romans 16:7, Andronicus and Junia are two men Paul names as "my kinsmen and fellow-prisoners." In Colossians 4:10, Aristarchus is called a "fellow-prisoner." These uses of the word prisoner seem to be meant literally. Taken literally in reference to Epaphras, Epaphras would be in chains with Paul in Rome for the crime of evangelism. Taken figuratively, Paul would be saying that Epaphras is as much committed to the gospel ministry

---

[19] (MacArthur 1992, 229)

as he is. Because Paul is freely sending him ahead to Philemon, it stands to reason that the second, figurative interpretation in this one instance is to be preferred.

Epaphras is also mentioned in Colossian 1:7 as a "fellow-servant, who is for you a faithful minister of Christ." I believe that we can take this to mean that Epaphras is a spiritual leader in the church at Colosse, but not the pastor. As I have discussed before, I believe there is more substance to the idea that Tychicus is the pastor of the church in Colosse (*Colossians 4:7 along with his name not being mentioned as continuing the journey to the church that is in Philemon's house*). Some have identified Epaphras as the pastor of the Philemon church due to these words. However, I have already identified Archippus as the pastor of Philemon's church. Since there is another house-church mentioned in Colossians 4:15-16 located in Laodicea, it may be that Epaphras is the pastor of that church meeting in the home of Nymphas. If that is the case, then Epaphras is to journey first to the church that meets in Philemon's house to help arrange Paul's accommodations, and then go on from there to Laodicea.

d. Supporting Companions of Paul

Phm 24 Μάρκος, Ἀρίσταρχος, Δημᾶς, Λουκᾶς, οἱ συνεργοί μου.

1. Mark

This is the same Mark mentioned in Acts 12:12. There, he is also identified by the name of John, Mary's son. He was the son of the Apostle Peter (*I Peter 5:13*). He was also the nephew to Barnabas (*Colossians 4:10*), who was Mary's brother and therefore Peter's brother-in-law. Paul and Barnabas took him on Paul's first missionary journey. He departed early from that trip which caused hard feelings between Paul and Mark. These feelings continued with the beginning of the second missionary trip that was being planned. Barnabas wanted to restore Mark, and Paul would not hear of it. It would have taken a lot to alienate Barnabas, known for his encouraging spirit, but the anger from Paul was too great. This friction resulted in Barnabas taking Mark and going to Cyprus, and Paul taking Silas and going towards Macedonia. Later on in life, Paul found the meaning of reconciliation. By the time of Paul's first imprisonment, he had made peace with Mark and was working with him again. Ray applies this act of reconciliation as an example to Philemon, "By mentioning Mark along with the others, though Mark had been somewhat strong minded before, Paul was showing how the grace of restoration works."[20]

---

[20] (Ray 2007, 218)

2. Aristarchus

Acts 19:29 identifies Aristarchus with a second man, Gaius, as men of Macedonia, and Paul's traveling companions. Acts 20:4 states that Aristarchus is from Thessalonica. Acts 27:2 tells us that Aristarchus sailed with Paul when Paul was being sent to Rome for his first imprisonment. He, too, would have been shipwrecked and incarcerated with Paul during the whole two years of house arrest. Colossians 4:10 identifies him as Paul's "fellow-prisoner." Obviously, Paul anticipated correctly not only his own freedom, but the freedom of his cell mate. He may have been freed by this time, which would have given Paul more opportunity to send letters to Colosse and the surrounding house-churches. It would have also given Paul more reason to expect a quick disposition of his own case.

3. Demas

This man is mentioned in a favorable light in only one other verse in scripture. Colossians 4:14 mentions him alongside of Luke. After the letters of Colossians and Philemon were written, Demas is seen as a deserter. In 2 Timothy 4:10, Paul mentions him predominately as someone who left him ". . . having loved this present world." Obviously, Demas didn't see his discomfort caused by serving the

Lord in difficult places as an investment in eternal treasures. This is in sharp contrast to the other men mentioned who endured to the end.

4. *Luke*

It is impossible to say too much about the "Beloved Physician." Suffice it here to say that Paul needed a doctor from time to time in his ministry. Paul's health was never good. Alas, Paul had a hard time with some of the personal relationships in his life, as well. Luke never deserted Paul. He served not only as his primary doctor, but also his best confidant. While Timothy is usually hailed as the heir-apparent of Paul's work, Luke seems content to chronicle the missionary movement for his part of the world. While it may be true that he served Paul's needs in distance places apart from the man, he never abandoned him. In 2 Timothy 4:11 Paul lovingly records that "only Luke is with me." I believe that Timothy and Luke were witnesses to Paul's last day on earth.

Paul identifies these people as his fellow-workers. This is the same designation that he gives to Philemon himself in verse 1. Taken together, these men served the Lord in the missionary movement of the first century. It is no small matter that, apart from Mark, these men were from the Hellenistic world. The gospel is for the whole world. What better ambassadors would there be for this message than those from this new world? Except for Demas, Paul surrounded himself with quality people. There is no great man of God without great men of God keeping his arms up in Christian mission.

e. Sincerely yours.

Phm 25 Ἡ χάρις το5 Κυρ5ου 5μῶν 5ησοῦ Χριστοῦ μετὰ τοῦ πνεύματος ὑμ5ν.,αμήν.

This ends the letter to Philemon. Just as it had begun, Paul invokes the grace of the Lord. This is a constant reminder that Jesus Christ is the controlling factor in our Christian lives. His Spirit is to be with our Spirit. This is the Spirit of the church depicted in the grand imagery of Jesus walking among the seven candlesticks in Revelation 2:1-3:22. The seventh of these letters is to the church in Laodicea. This church is in such close proximity, that we can easily see the church at Colosse and her sister church meeting at Philemon's house as also being addressed. Philemon had wealth, and had obviously shared that wealth. He was, after all, a giving man. The Laodicean church was known for its great material wealth.

However, there is a warning here in Revelation that may pertain to that church. Jesus would tell that church that because they were lukewarm that He would spew them out of His mouth. Part of being spiritually dead is not realizing that the Spirit is never just a vague, warm feeling. Philemon needed to keep that fact constant in his thoughts. He serves a living Lord. The church is revived by that confession of faith. We don't really know what happened next in Philemon's life. I believe that he would be as the overcomer in Revelation 3:21, as he opened his heart to the Lordship of Jesus Christ and became reconciled to Onesimus. The existence of this letter testifies to the happy conclusion that must have come. If Philemon had refused Paul's instruction, then the letter would become a distraction to the work being done around Colosse and Ephesus. Philemon, himself, would become a pariah in the church. Matthew Henry states eloquently in conclusion:

> "We, like Onesimus, were revolters from God's service, and had injured him in his right. Jesus Christ finds us, and by his grace works a change in us, and then intercedes for us with the Father, that we may be received into his favour and family again, and past offences may be forgiven; and we are sure that the Father heareth him always; There is no reason to doubt but Paul prevailed with Philemon to forgive and receive Onesimus: and more reason have we to be confident that the intercession of Christ with the Father is prevalent for the acceptance of all whose case he takes in hand and recommends to him."[21]

---

[21] *Matthew Henry's Commentary*, s.v. "Philemon."

APPENDIX A.

Personal translation of the book of Philemon. Not to be used in public worship.

Paul, a prisoner of Christ Jesus, and the brother Timothy, to beloved Philemon, our fellow-laborer. And to beloved Apphia, and Archippus, our fellow-soldier, and to the ones with the church in your house. Grace to you (pl) and peace from God our Father, our Lord Jesus Christ. I give thanks to my God, always remembering to make my prayers to God of you. Hearing of your love and faith which you hold for the Lord Jesus, and towards all the holy ones. That the partnership of your faith becomes powerful in knowing all the goodness that is in you (pl) on account of Christ Jesus.

For we have much joy and comfort in your (sg) love (agape), that the bowels (tender emotions what we would say as the "heart") of the holy ones are refreshed by you (sg), brother. Wherefore, with much boldness in Christ I could command you to a duty. By means of more love I encourage you, in the character of Paul the aged, and at this moment the prisoner of Jesus Christ. I encourage you about my son, the one born in my imprisonment, Onesimus. Who once was worthless to you, but now precious to you and to me. Who I myself have sent to you (sg), he that is in my bowels (heart), receive him in. Who I desired to keep with me, in order that in your place he could serve me in the prison of the gospel. But without your judgment, I desire to do nothing, in order that your benefit is not because of your need, but because of your desire.

Perhaps he departed for a time, so that you can have him back for all time. No longer as a slave, but beyond a slave, a loved brother, especially to me. How much more to you, both in the flesh and in the Lord? Therefore, if you count me as a partner, receive him in (vs. 12) as you would me. But if he has wronged you in something, or owes you anything, put that thing to my account. I Paul have written by my own will, I will repay it however I do not say to you, "you owe yourself to me" Truly, brother, let me be helped from you in the Lord, refresh (vs. 7) my bowels (heart) in the Lord. Having been persuaded of your obedience, I wrote to you, knowing that even more than I say, you will do.

But, at the same time make the necessary preparations for me to be housed, for because of your (pl) prayers I shall by grace be restored to you (pl). Welcome Epaphras my fellow-prisoner in Christ Jesus. Mark, Aristarchus, Demas, Luke, my fellow-workers.

The grace of our Lord Jesus Christ be with your Spirit. Amen.

APPENDIX B.

Opening address identifications of Paul as found in his 12 books of the NT.

Romans—Paul, a servant of Jesus Christ

I Cor.—Paul, called to be an apostle of Jesus Christ

II Cor.—Paul, an apostle of Jesus Christ

Gal.—Paul, an apostle

Eph.—Paul, an apostle of Jesus Christ

Phil.—Paul. . .the servants of Jesus Christ

Col.—Paul, an apostle of Jesus Christ

I Thes.—Paul. . .(without designation)

II Thes.—Paul. . .(without designation)

I Tim.—Paul, an apostle of Jesus Christ

II Tim.—Paul, an apostle of Jesus Christ

Titus—Paul, a servant of God and an apostle of Jesus Christ

APPENDIX C.

Sermon: From Slave to Beloved Brother

We turn to the small book of Philemon. For those of you who are unfamiliar with it because there's not a lot of sermons that are traditionally come out of this book, being only twenty-five verses long, it's in the New Testament about two-thirds of the way through. It is actually in the last book of the collected works of Paul: I Timothy, II Timothy, Titus, Philemon, and in that order.

Let me tell you the story a little bit. It's about a man by the name of Onesimus. I have to mention that four-dollar word because that is whom the story is about. Onesimus was a runaway. The overwhelming tradition, I'll say that again clearly, the overwhelming *tradition* of Onesimus is that he was a runaway slave. His master's name was Philemon. According to the overwhelming tradition passed down through these generations to us today, Philemon was the master, Onesimus was the slave, and the slave stole money from Philemon and had run off. As an escaped slave, he headed towards the west, hit Ephesus, got himself a boat, and wound up smack-dab in the middle of Rome. There in Rome, he met the Apostle Paul who was in prison. Paul was approximately somewhere around sixty years old. Paul had been in prison a year or more of a two year prison term that he was going to spend at that point in his life. He was in prison before, and he was going to be in prison after this. Paul was in the middle of writing many of the books of the Bible that we have collected for us today. He was preaching, unfettered and unchained, to anyone who had come into the house that Paul had opportunity to rent. He was under what we would call today "House Arrest."

According to the long standing tradition, Onesimus came and sat at Paul's feet and was converted--he found the Lord. Sometime after that experience, before not too horribly long, Onesimus came to himself and said, "I have to make this right, but I don't know how." Then, according to the long standing tradition, Paul wrote a letter to Philemon requesting Philemon that he accepts his slave back, not to beat him, and not to punish him. He was coming back with a new spirit, coming back as a new person; Philemon was to receive him as a brother.

I will start in verse 15 and read through verses 16 and 17. In those three verses we find the crux of the matter, we find the core of this great and little book. I say "great" because this is a tremendous book of the Bible; there is so much here. However, I going to go against the tradition of the centuries, and I'm going to give you what I feel is the truth. You're not going to find this in any other book. You're not going to find this on the internet. You're not going to find this anywhere except me. I am the lone voice crying in the wilderness what I think is the correct interpretation of this book of Philemon.

Am I right? I am as right as anyone who would call Onesimus a slave. I am as right as any of the two thousand years of tradition that has been brought down because everything that I just told you as tradition has been formulated as a result of twenty-five verses where the word "Slave" has been applied to Onesimus only in verse 16 twice. "Slave" with the Apostle Paul could actually be figurative. Paul called himself a slave, he does that many times, but he does that figuratively. There's about twenty-nine times that the Apostle Paul uses the word slave in his writings; of those, well over half are used figuratively as someone who is "sold-out" to the Lord--someone who is committed entirely to the Lord.

I'm going to twist the book of Philemon a little bit so that it makes a greater application, and I have reasons for it that I don't have opportunity and time to share, and scholarly reasons why I think I could and will do this. Suffice it to say this is a tremendous story of love, hurt, and reconciliation.

Let me ask you this question, "Have you ever run away from home?" I have when I was a kid. I ran away from home, at least that what my folks told me I did. In reality all I did was leave the house when I was three or four years old. We lived in a mill town that had a railroad train that often ran back and forth through the town carrying big cords of lumber to the paper mill. They also carried a lot of oil for fuel. Trains at that early age fascinated me. I remember one particular afternoon my mom was downstairs doing the ironing and I was upstairs. I looked around and I didn't see where she was. I just kind of "bee-bopped" down the stairs and out the front door, down the street, down the hill, and went downtown. I went behind the local grocery store and just sat there on the side of a little hill just to look at the train. I sat there for two or three hours just to look at the train. After two or three hours just looking at the train, I walked back downtown, climbed back up the hill, and it was getting a little bit dark. I walked back in the house. My dad was home, my mom was home, my big brother was home, and my big sister was home. I had run away from home. I didn't even know that I had run away. I knew where I was the whole time. I know what it is to be a runaway.

Maybe as a parent you know what it is to have a runaway. If you've ever had your child run away from home, how does that feel? Oh my goodness, what a shock, what a pit in your stomach, what agony, what frustration. Is this child dead or alive? Is this child ok or is this child in a ditch? Has someone kidnapped this child? Has this child run in front of traffic? There are all sorts of frantic thoughts and we always think the worst. We never think this child is just down at the railroad tracks just to watch the trains.

Let me tell you what I think this story of Philemon is about. Philemon is about a runaway. Onesimus was a runaway. But I believe, as I study this book and I look at the words, that Philemon was

Onesimus's son--his blood. Onesimus ran away from home like the Prodigal Son in Luke 15. I do not know if he stole a dime, and nobody knows for sure that he took a penny. But as we read, he did do something serious wrong. Philemon was mad, upset, and frustrated. You're not going to get this frustrated, as the words contained in this book, with just a slave. Paul is not going to write the words of reconciliation that he's going to write to Philemon for a slave; but he will for a son.

Let's read this passage:

> Philemon 15-17. **For perhaps he** *(Onesimus)* **therefore departed for a season, that thou shouldest receive him forever. Not now as a servant, but above a servant, a brother beloved, specially to me, but how much more unto thee, both in the flesh, and in the Lord? If thou count me therefore a partner, receive him as myself.**

These three verses form the very pivotal core of this book; this short little letter. In verse 15, Paul first of all tries to give a reason for someone running away from home. It's not just an emotional outcry; it's not something outrageous or violent. He said, "Philemon, there could be a reason to this. I accept and understand your anger, but you are better than this, Philemon. Your reputation precedes you as a giver, someone who supports the church, encourages the church, and houses the church. Now this crisis has happened." No greater crisis could happen than a man loses his son by running away. No greater tearing at a man's soul than realizing his son has left in the middle of the night and not says a word. Paul was encouraging, "Maybe it was because there was a reason behind it that he left you for a little bit, a season. Maybe he left you for that brief moment because there is something in store for him and for you." He said, "This is the reason: he left for a little bit so that now he can be returned to you for all eternity because there has been a change." There is something that is different now.

There has been a moment in his life that has made all the difference in the world. Read verse 16: "Not now as a servant. . ." again, I believe "Servant" to be a symbolic term. Not just somebody who has to have his head hung down low. Not just somebody who as the Prodigal Son said, in the middle of the pig sty, "My father has his servants eating better than me. Maybe I can go back and say, 'Dear dad, can I come back as your servant because you know I can't come back as your son.'" That was the mindset going on in the Prodigal Son of Luke 15. Now, here with Paul, Dr. Luke is over in the corner laughing because he's heard this story before. Paul now says, "You're not going to receive him as a servant, but you're going to receive him as a brother beloved."

I said that Onesimus was Philemon's son. Why didn't Paul say that he was going to be his son again? I'll explain that in a moment, there is a very good reason for that. He said, "Receive him, not as a servant, but as a beloved brother." There is a key word in there, "*Beloved* brother." Look around, we are the brethren. It's not a correct word but we are the "Sisterren." We are the family. Do you love one another? We need to love one another. We need to receive one another as brothers and sisters in Christ. Not as a tool. There's nobody here that anyone can use and abuse because we are brothers and sisters in Christ.

"You are not to receive him as a servant, but above a servant, a *beloved* brother." The word, love, is used six times in this little, short book—six times. You know what else is used six times; the word, "Lord." "Beloved brother, especially to me, because he's been here with me. But how much more unto you; both in the flesh and in the Lord--in reality and in spirituality." The Lordship of Jesus Christ takes over. You want to know how Onesimus can make these changes? You want to know how he can go from a runaway for a season to one who can be received for all eternity? It's because of the Lord. That makes all the difference in the world. The Lord Jesus Christ put that change in his life.

Paul goes on to admonish Philemon, "If you count me therefore a partner, if I'm one and the same to you, if we are joined at the hip, if we work together in the faith, then receive Onesimus just as you would receive me." Why not call Onesimus a son in verse 16? It is because Onesimus's life had changed. His father is now God. When the head of your life becomes God, then we now become brothers and sisters together. When the Lord is master and savior of your life, we become family. That's why I believe Paul wrote to Philemon and said, "He's not your son anymore, he's God's son."

So, folks, how do we apply this? Simply and absolutely. We look around and we see a lot of runaways, maybe in our own homes, or maybe we have friends and family members who have experienced the runaways. I never once thought that I was a runaway, not one time. That didn't change how my mom and dad felt about me that day, and they let me know about it through their grief, worry, and frustration. But then they also finally rejoiced when I returned safe and sound. We can look around and we can see spiritual runaways. People who receive the call of God in their heart, and turn and walk away; people who say, "No" to God, "I don't care what You say, I'm going to live my own life in my own way." This person is a runaway from God. What changes a runaway into a brother or sister? The Lord Jesus Christ comes into that heart. The hurt is gone. That's gone because Jesus Christ makes it gone. That's gone because He paid the price, went to the cross, and gave us eternal life. Yes, while we may be runaways for a time, we can come back to Him; and now be received as brothers and sisters in Christ for all eternity. That sure beats that little snapshot of time that we ran away.

Then what are we to do? We, as a family and as a church, harken back to verse 17. When this one comes back then we are going to throw it back in his face every time we see him. We are going to remind him of how much he made us hurt. We will do that because we have learned how to do it really well. But, we can't do *that* any longer. When that person who has run away returns, they will see open arms and open heart; because we know that Jesus Christ has changed that life—from a servant to a brother. Jesus Christ transforms the life.

This morning, I encourage you, if you haven't seen that transformation in your own life; you may be that runaway we've been talking about. Maybe, you're the Onesimus today. You maybe exiled somewhere asking, "How am I supposed to get back? What am I supposed to say? Is it even possible?" Yes! It is possible. You can be changed, transformed, and restored. You can be received into the family of God. Accept the love of the Lord Jesus Christ and be changed.

BIBLIOGRAPHY

Barclay, William. *The Letters to Timothy, Titus, and Philemon.* Louisville: Westminster John Knox Press, 2003.

Buttrick, George A. "Exposition of Philemon." In *The Interpreter's Bible*. Nashville: Abingdon Press, 1955.

Guthrie, Donald. *The Pastoral Epistles.* Grand Rapids: Wm. B. Eerdmans Publishing Company, 1990.

Henry, Matthew. "Philemon." In *Matthew Henry's Commentary Vol. VI*, by Matthew Henry. Old Tappan: Fleming H. Revell Company, n.d.

Ironside, H.A. *1 and 2 Timothy, Titus, and Philemon.* Grand Rapids: Kregel Publication, 2008.

Knox, John. "Introduction to Philemon." In *The Interpreter's Bible*. Nashville: Abingdon Press, 1955.

MacArthur, John. *Colossians and Philemon.* Chicago: Moody Publishers, 1992.

McGee, J. Vernon. *First and Second Timothy, Titus, Philemon.* Nashville: Thomas Nelson Publishers, 1991.

Phillips, John. *Exploring Colossians and Philemon.* Grand Rapids: Kregel Publications, 2002.

Ray, Charles. *The Books of First and Second Timothy, Titus, and Philemon.* Chattanooga: AMG Publishers, 2007.

Stedman, Ray C. "Philemon: A Brother Restored." *Adventuring through the Bible*, 1968: Message Number 58.

Made in the USA
Middletown, DE
19 December 2022

19599433R00057